Book and CD for B♭, E♭ and C Instruments

Arranged and Produced by Mark Taylor

T0071734

BOOK

CD

Cover photo: Frank Driggs Collection

ISBN 978-0-634-07991-7

7777 W. BLUEMOUND RD. P.O. BOX 13819 MILWAUKEE, WI 53213

Horace Silver

Volume 36

Arranged and Produced by
Mark Taylor

Featured Players:

Graham Breedlove–Trumpet
John Desalme–Tenor Sax
Tony Nalker–Piano
Jim Roberts–Bass
Steve Fidyk–Drums

HOW TO USE THE CD:

Each song has two tracks:

1) Split Track/Melody

Woodwind, Brass, Keyboard, and **Mallet Players** can use this track as a learning tool for melody style and inflection.

Bass Players can learn and perform with this track – remove the recorded bass track by turning down the volume on the LEFT channel.

Keyboard and **Guitar Players** can learn and perform with this track – remove the recorded piano part by turning down the volume on the RIGHT channel.

2) Full Stereo Track

Soloists or **Groups** can learn and perform with this accompaniment track with the RHYTHM SECTION only.

CD
1 : SPLIT TRACK/MELODY
2 : FULL STEREO TRACK
DOODLIN'
WORDS AND MUSIC BY
HORACE SILVER
C VERSION
MEDIUM SWING
Db7
mf
Gb7
Db7
Fmi7 Bb7
Ebmi7
Ab7
1.
Db7
Ab7
2.
Db7
TO CODA
Ab7
Db6
Gb6
Db6
Ebmi7
Ab7
Db6
SOLO (5 CHORUSES)
Db7
Gb7
Db7
Abmi7 Db7
Gb7
D.S. AL CODA
TAKE REPEAT
Db7
Fmi7 Bb7
Ebmi7
Ab7
Db7
Ebmi7 Ab7
CODA
G9(#11)

THE JODY GRIND

NICA'S DREAM

C VERSION

WORDS AND MUSIC BY
HORACE SILVER

MEDIUM LATIN

RHYTHM

PLAY

SWING

LATIN

Abmi7
Db7
Abmi7
Db7
3
Gbma7 Db7
C7(#9)
B/F
TO CODA
F+7
Bbmi(ma7)
SOLO
Bbmi(ma7)
Abmi(ma7)
Bbmi(ma7)
Abmi7
Db7
Abmi7
Db7
Gbma7
C7(#9)
B/F
F+7
Bbmi(ma7)
SWING
Ebmi7/Ab
Ab7(b9)
Dbma7
Bb7
Eb9(#11)
Ab7
Dbma9
Emi9
A7
Ebmi7/Ab
Ab7(b9)
Dbma7
Bb7
Eb9(#11)
Ab7
Dbma7
F+7(b9)
LATIN
Bbmi(ma7)
Abmi(ma7)
Bbmi(ma7)
Abmi7
Db7
Abmi7
Db7
Gbma7
C7(#9)
B/F
F+7
Bbmi(ma7)
D.S. AL CODA
PLAY
mf
CODA
F+7
Bbmi(ma7)

CD

7 : SPLIT TRACK/MELODY

8 : FULL STEREO TRACK

OPUS DE FUNK

WORDS AND MUSIC BY
HORACE SILVER

C VERSION

CD
9 : SPLIT TRACK/MELODY
10 : FULL STEREO TRACK
C VERSION
PEACE
WORDS AND MUSIC BY
HORACE SILVER
SLOW BALLAD
AMI7(b5) Ab9 GMI7 C7(b9) BMA7 CMI7(b5) F+7(#9)
mf
BbMA7 BMI7 E9 AMA7 F#MI7
TO CODA
EbMI7(b5) Ab13 Ab+7 DbMA7 C7(b5) B7(b5)
1. BbMA7
2. BbMA7
SOLO
AMI7(b5) Ab9 GMI7 C7(b9) BMA7 CMI7(b5) F+7(#9)
BbMA7 BMI7 E9 AMA7 F#MI7
D.S. AL CODA
EbMI7(b5) Ab13 Ab+7 DbMA7 C7(b5) B7(b5) BbMA7
mf
CODA
BbMA9

THE PREACHER

WORDS AND MUSIC BY
HORACE SILVER

SISTER SADIE

CD
15 : SPLIT TRACK/MELODY
16 : FULL STEREO TRACK

WORDS AND MUSIC BY
HORACE SILVER

C VERSION

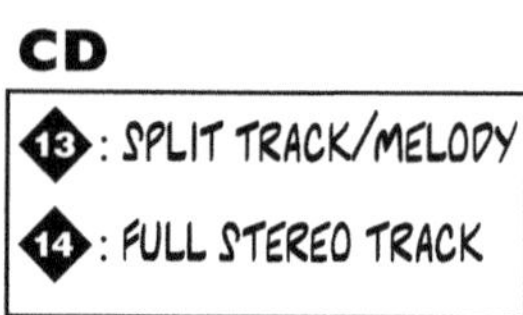

CD

13 : SPLIT TRACK/MELODY

14 : FULL STEREO TRACK

SEÑOR BLUES

WORDS AND MUSIC BY
HORACE SILVER

C VERSION

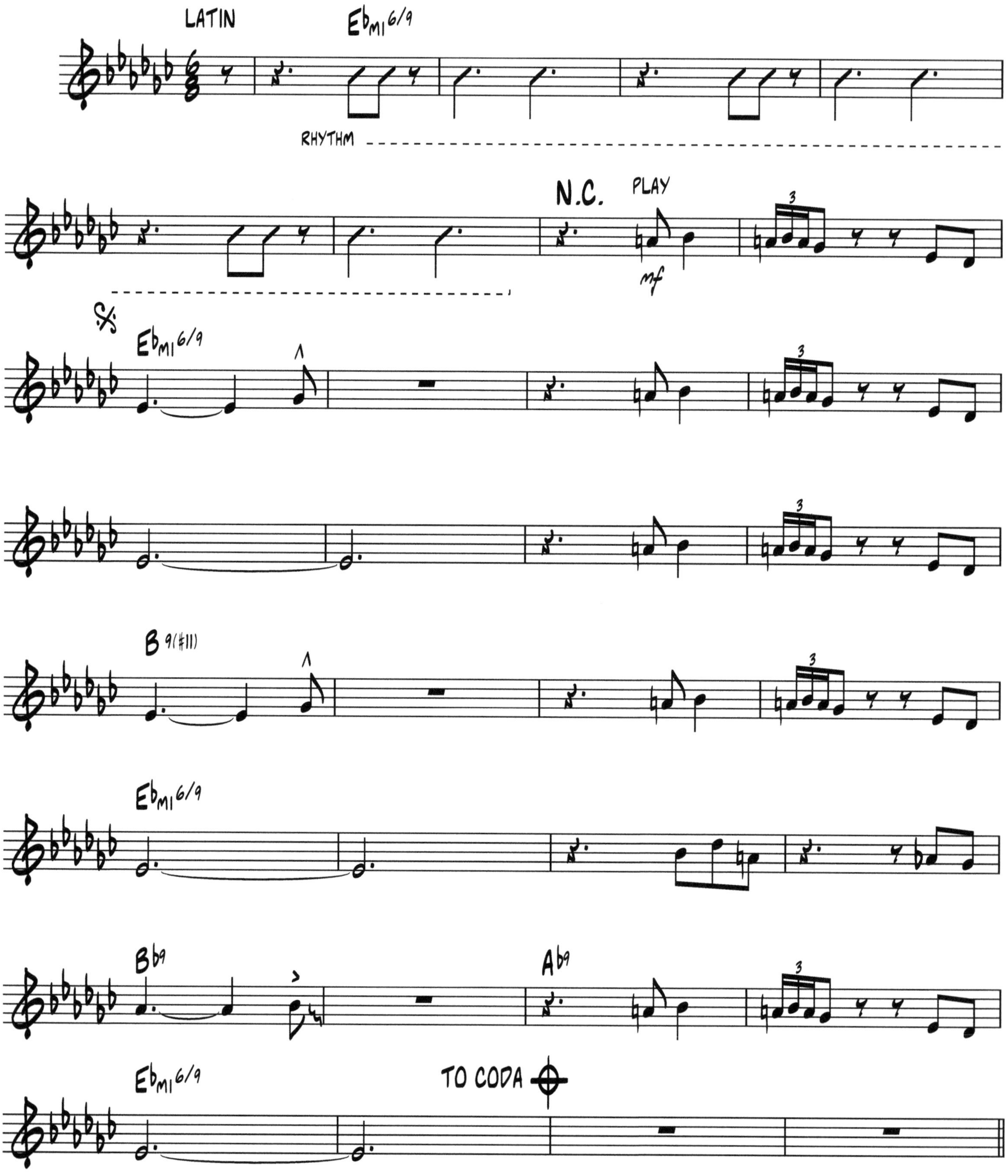

LATIN
E♭MI6/9
RHYTHM
N.C.
PLAY
mf
E♭MI6/9
B9(♯11)
E♭MI6/9
B♭9
A♭9
E♭MI6/9
TO CODA

SOLO
Ebmi6/9
B9(#11)
Ebmi6/9
Bb13
Ab13
Ebmi6/9
1., 2.
3.
PLAY
mf
3
D.S. AL CODA
CODA
Ebmi6/9
RHYTHM

CD

17 : SPLIT TRACK/MELODY

18 : FULL STEREO TRACK

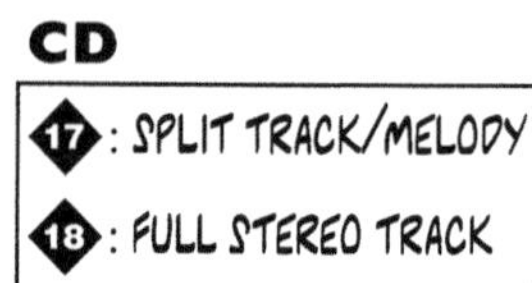

SONG FOR MY FATHER

C VERSION

WORDS AND MUSIC BY
HORACE SILVER

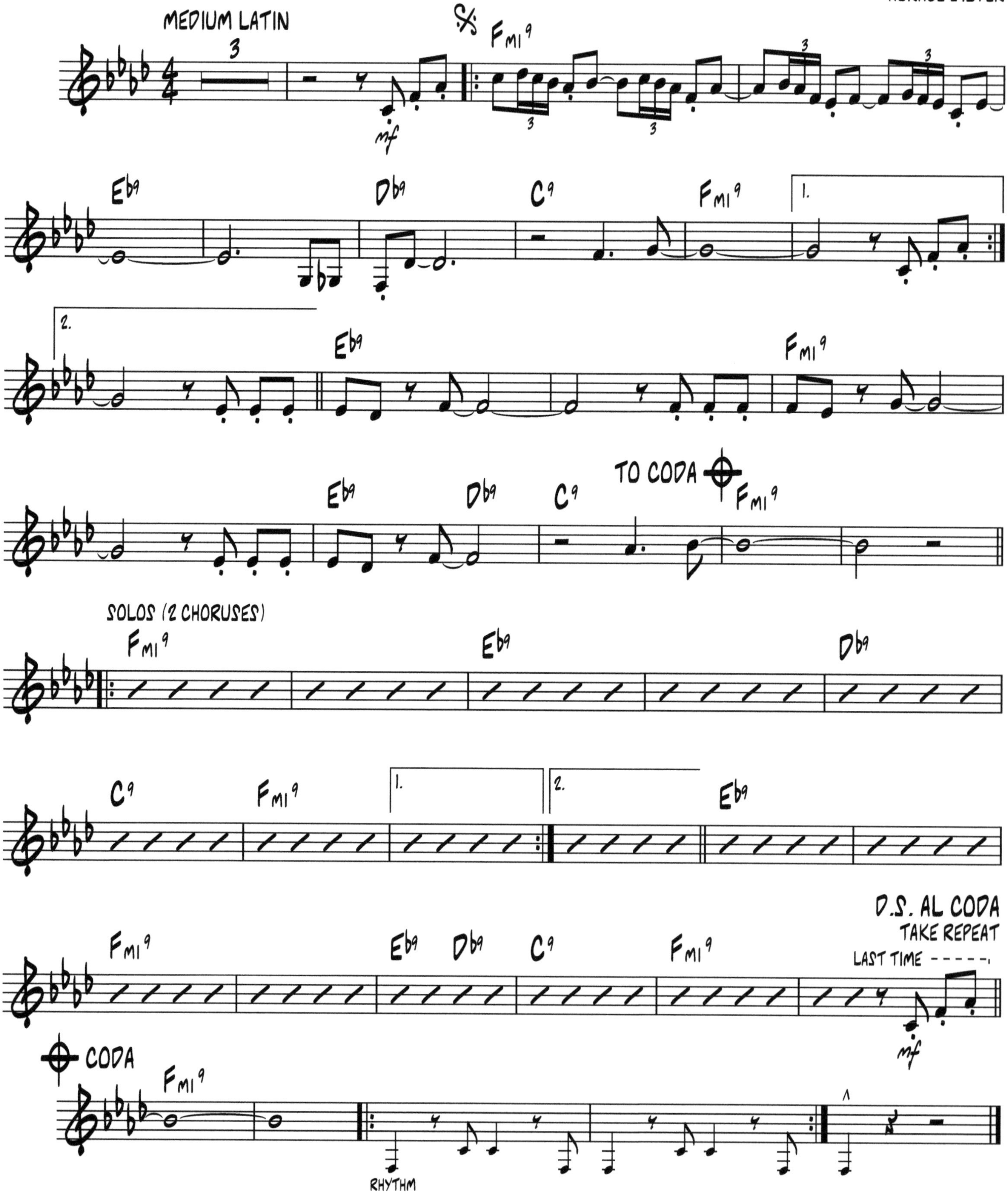

MEDIUM LATIN
3
mf
FMI9
Eb9
Db9
C9
FMI9
1.
2.
Eb9
FMI9
Eb9
Db9
C9
TO CODA
FMI9
SOLOS (2 CHORUSES)
FMI9
Eb9
Db9
C9
FMI9
1.
2.
Eb9
FMI9
Eb9
Db9
C9
FMI9
D.S. AL CODA
TAKE REPEAT
LAST TIME
mf
CODA
FMI9
RHYTHM

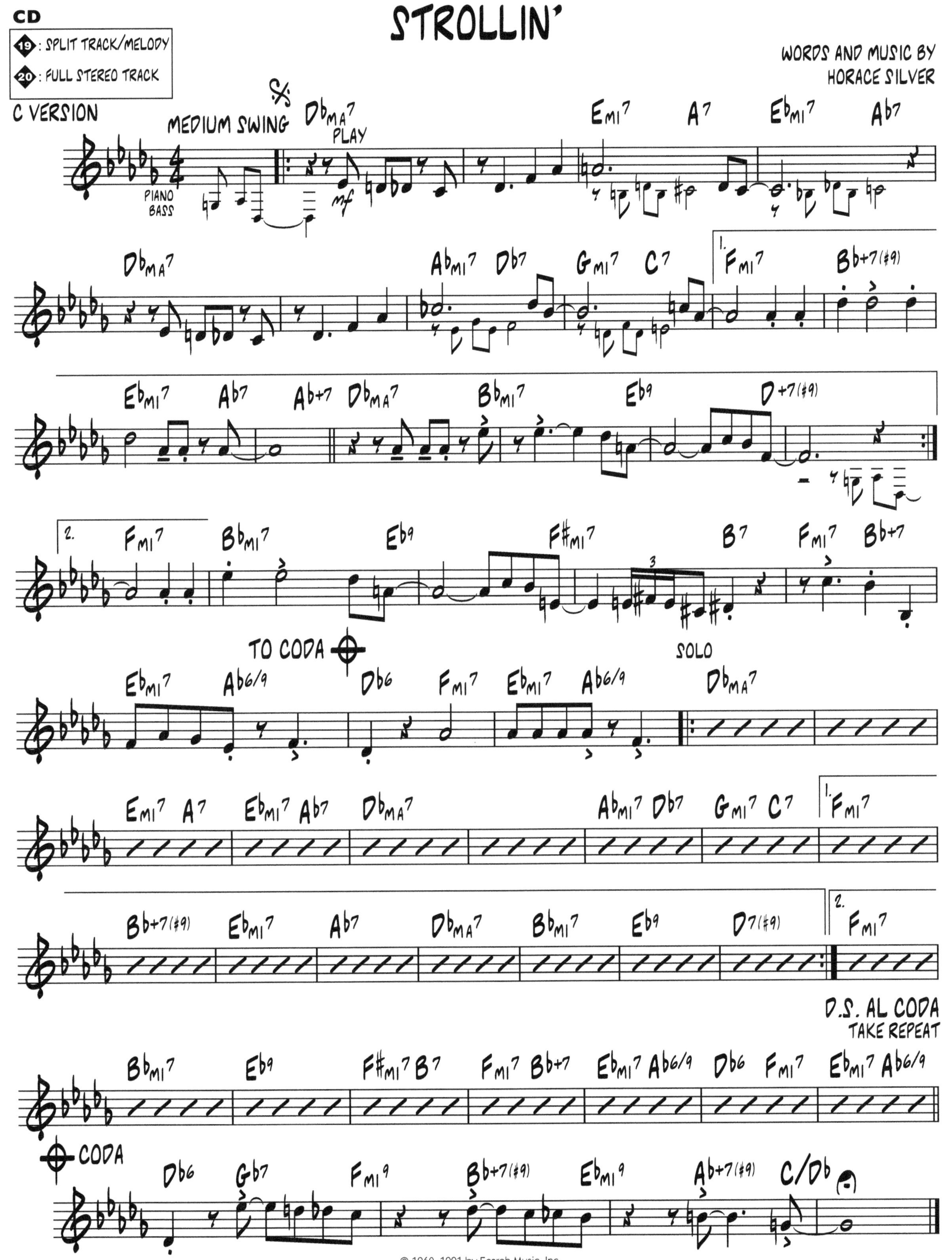
CD
19 : SPLIT TRACK/MELODY
20 : FULL STEREO TRACK
STROLLIN'
WORDS AND MUSIC BY
HORACE SILVER
C VERSION
MEDIUM SWING
PLAY
PIANO
BASS
Dbma7 Emi7 A7 Ebmi7 Ab7
Dbma7 Abmi7 Db7 Gmi7 C7 Fmi7 Bb+7(#9)
Ebmi7 Ab7 Ab+7 Dbma7 Bbmi7 Eb9 D+7(#9)
Fmi7 Bbmi7 Eb9 F#mi7 B7 Fmi7 Bb+7
TO CODA
SOLO
Ebmi7 Ab6/9 Db6 Fmi7 Ebmi7 Ab6/9 Dbma7
Emi7 A7 Ebmi7 Ab7 Dbma7 Abmi7 Db7 Gmi7 C7 Fmi7
Bb+7(#9) Ebmi7 Ab7 Dbma7 Bbmi7 Eb9 D7(#9) Fmi7
D.S. AL CODA
TAKE REPEAT
Bbmi7 Eb9 F#mi7 B7 Fmi7 Bb+7 Ebmi7 Ab6/9 Db6 Fmi7 Ebmi7 Ab6/9
CODA
Db6 Gb7 Fmi9 Bb+7(#9) Ebmi9 Ab+7(#9) C/Db

CD

1: SPLIT TRACK/MELODY
2: FULL STEREO TRACK

DOODLIN'

WORDS AND MUSIC BY
HORACE SILVER

B♭ VERSION

CD
3 : SPLIT TRACK/MELODY
4 : FULL STEREO TRACK
THE JODY GRIND
WORDS AND MUSIC BY
HORACE SILVER
Bb VERSION
FUNKY
CMI7
F9
CMI7
B9(b5)
TO CODA
C#9(b5)
CMI7
SOLOS (7 CHORUSES)
CMI7
F9
CMI7
B9(b5)
C#9(b5)
CMI7
D.S. AL CODA
TAKE REPEAT
LAST TIME
CODA
CMI7

CD

NICA'S DREAM

WORDS AND MUSIC BY
HORACE SILVER

B♭ VERSION

MEDIUM LATIN

Cmi(ma7) Bbmi(ma7) Cmi(ma7) Bbmi(ma7) PLAY

RHYTHM

mf

Cmi(ma7) Bbmi(ma7) Cmi(ma7)

Bbmi7 Eb7 Bbmi7 Eb7 Abma7 Eb7 D7(#9)

C#/G G+7 Cmi(ma7) 1. 2.

SWING

Fmi9/Bb Bb7(b9) Ebma7 C7

F9(#11) Bb7 D7(#9)/Eb F#mi9 B7

Fmi9/Bb Bb7(b9) Ebma7 C7

F9(#11) Bb7 D7(#9)/Eb G+7(b9)

LATIN

Cmi(ma7) Bbmi(ma7) Cmi(ma7)

Bb MI7
Eb7
Bb MI7
Eb7
TO CODA
Ab MA7
Eb7
D7(#9)
C#/G
G+7
C MI(MA7)
SOLO
C MI(MA7)
Bb MI(MA7)
C MI(MA7)
Bb MI7
Eb7
Bb MI7
Eb7
Ab MA7
D7(#9)
C#/G
G+7
C MI(MA7)
SWING
F MI7/Bb
Bb7(b9)
Eb MA7
C7
F9(#11)
Bb7
Eb MA9
F# MI9
B7
F MI7/Bb
Bb7(b9)
Eb MA7
C7
F9(#11)
Bb7
Eb MA7
G+7(b9)
LATIN
C MI(MA7)
Bb MI(MA7)
C MI(MA7)
Bb MI7
Eb7
Bb MI7
Eb7
Ab MA7
D7(#9)
C#/G
G+7
C MI(MA7)
D.S. AL CODA
PLAY
mf
CODA
G+7
C MI(MA7)

OPUS DE FUNK

CD
7 : SPLIT TRACK/MELODY
8 : FULL STEREO TRACK
Bb VERSION
MEDIUM JAZZ
WORDS AND MUSIC BY
HORACE SILVER
C6
C7
F7
F#o7
C6/G
Emi7 A7
Dmi7
G7
C6
C6
E7
Ami7
Ab+7
Gmi7
C7
F7
F#o7
C6/G
Emi7 A7
Dmi7
G7
C6
FINE
SOLO (9 CHORUSES)
C6
Dmi7 G7
C6
Gmi7 C7
F7
F#o7
C6
Emi7 A7
Dmi7
G7
C6
D.S. AL FINE
Dmi7 G7

CD
9 : SPLIT TRACK/MELODY
10 : FULL STEREO TRACK
Bb VERSION
PEACE
WORDS AND MUSIC BY
HORACE SILVER
SLOW BALLAD
mf
Bmi7(b5) Bb9 Ami7 D7(b9) C#ma7 Dmi7(b5) G+7(#9)
Cma7 C#mi7 F#9 Bma7 G#mi7
Fmi7(b5) Bb13 Bb+7 Ebma7 D7(b5) C#7(b5)
TO CODA
1. Cma7
2. Cma7
SOLO
Bmi7(b5) Bb9 Ami7 D7(b9) C#ma7 Dmi7(b5) G+7(#9)
Cma7 C#mi7 F#9 Bma7 G#mi7
D.S. AL CODA
Fmi7(b5) Bb13 Bb+7 Ebma7 D7(b5) C#7(b5) Cma7
mf
CODA
Cma9

CD
11 : SPLIT TRACK/MELODY
12 : FULL STEREO TRACK
THE PREACHER
WORDS AND MUSIC BY
HORACE SILVER
B♭ VERSION
SWING
mf
TO CODA
SOLO
D.S. AL CODA
TAKE REPEAT
PLAY
mf
CODA

SISTER SADIE
CD
15 : SPLIT TRACK/MELODY
16 : FULL STEREO TRACK
WORDS AND MUSIC BY
HORACE SILVER
Bb VERSION
MEDIUM BLUES
Bb13
A13
mf
RHYTHM
1.
2.
TO CODA
SOLO (3 CHORUSES)
D13
C13
B13
D.S. AL CODA
TAKE REPEAT
CODA
D7 C#7 C7 B7
C7 B7 Bb7 A7

CD
13: SPLIT TRACK/MELODY
14: FULL STEREO TRACK

Bb VERSION

SEÑOR BLUES

WORDS AND MUSIC BY
HORACE SILVER

SOLO
FMI6/9
C#9(#11)
FMI6/9
C13
Bb13
FMI6/9
1., 2.
3.
PLAY
mf
D.S. AL CODA
CODA
FMI6/9
RHYTHM

CD

17 : SPLIT TRACK/MELODY
18 : FULL STEREO TRACK

B♭ VERSION

SONG FOR MY FATHER

WORDS AND MUSIC BY
HORACE SILVER

CD
19 : SPLIT TRACK/MELODY
20 : FULL STEREO TRACK
STROLLIN'
WORDS AND MUSIC BY
HORACE SILVER
Bb VERSION
MEDIUM SWING
PLAY
PIANO
BASS
Eb MA7
F#MI7 B7 FMI7 Bb7
Eb MA7
BbMI7 Eb7 AMI7 D7
1. GMI7 C+7(#9)
FMI7 Bb7 Bb+7 Eb MA7 CMI7 F9 E+7(#9)
2. GMI7 CMI7 F9 G#MI7 C#7 GMI7 C+7
TO CODA
SOLO
FMI7 Bb6/9 Eb6 GMI7 FMI7 Bb6/9 Eb MA7
F#MI7 B7 FMI7 Bb7 Eb MA7 BbMI7 Eb7 AMI7 D7 1. GMI7
C+7(#9) FMI7 Bb7 Eb MA7 CMI7 F9 E7(#9) 2. GMI7
D.S. AL CODA
TAKE REPEAT
CMI7 F9 G#MI7 C#7 GMI7 C+7 FMI7 Bb6/9 Eb6 GMI7 FMI7 Bb6/9
CODA
Eb6 Ab7 GMI9 C+7(#9) FMI9 Bb+7(#9) D/Eb

CD

DOODLIN'

1 : SPLIT TRACK/MELODY
2 : FULL STEREO TRACK
WORDS AND MUSIC BY
HORACE SILVER
Eb VERSION
MEDIUM SWING
Bb7
mf
Eb7
Bb7
Dmi7 G7
Cmi7
F7
1.
Bb7
F7
2.
Bb7
TO CODA
F7
Bb6
Eb6
Bb6
Cmi7
F7
Bb6
SOLO (5 CHORUSES)
Bb7
Eb7
Bb7
Fmi7 Bb7
Eb7
D.S. AL CODA
TAKE REPEAT
Bb7
Dmi7 G7
Cmi7
F7
Bb7
Cmi7 F7
CODA
E9(#11)

CD
3 : SPLIT TRACK/MELODY
4 : FULL STEREO TRACK
THE JODY GRIND
WORDS AND MUSIC BY
HORACE SILVER
Eb VERSION
FUNKY
Gmi7
mf
C9
Gmi7
F#9(b5)
G#9(b5)
Gmi7
TO CODA
1.
2.
SOLOS (7 CHORUSES)
Gmi7
C9
Gmi7
F#9(b5)
G#9(b5)
Gmi7
D.S. AL CODA
TAKE REPEAT
LAST TIME
CODA
Gmi7

CD

5 : SPLIT TRACK/MELODY

6 : FULL STEREO TRACK

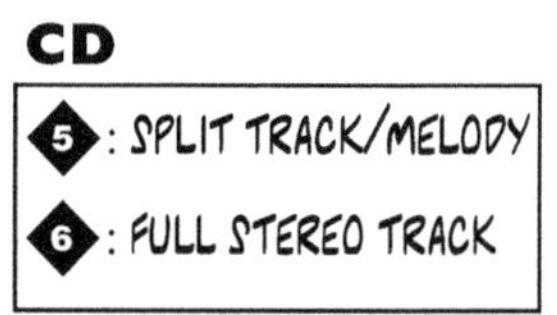

NICA'S DREAM

WORDS AND MUSIC BY
HORACE SILVER

Eb VERSION

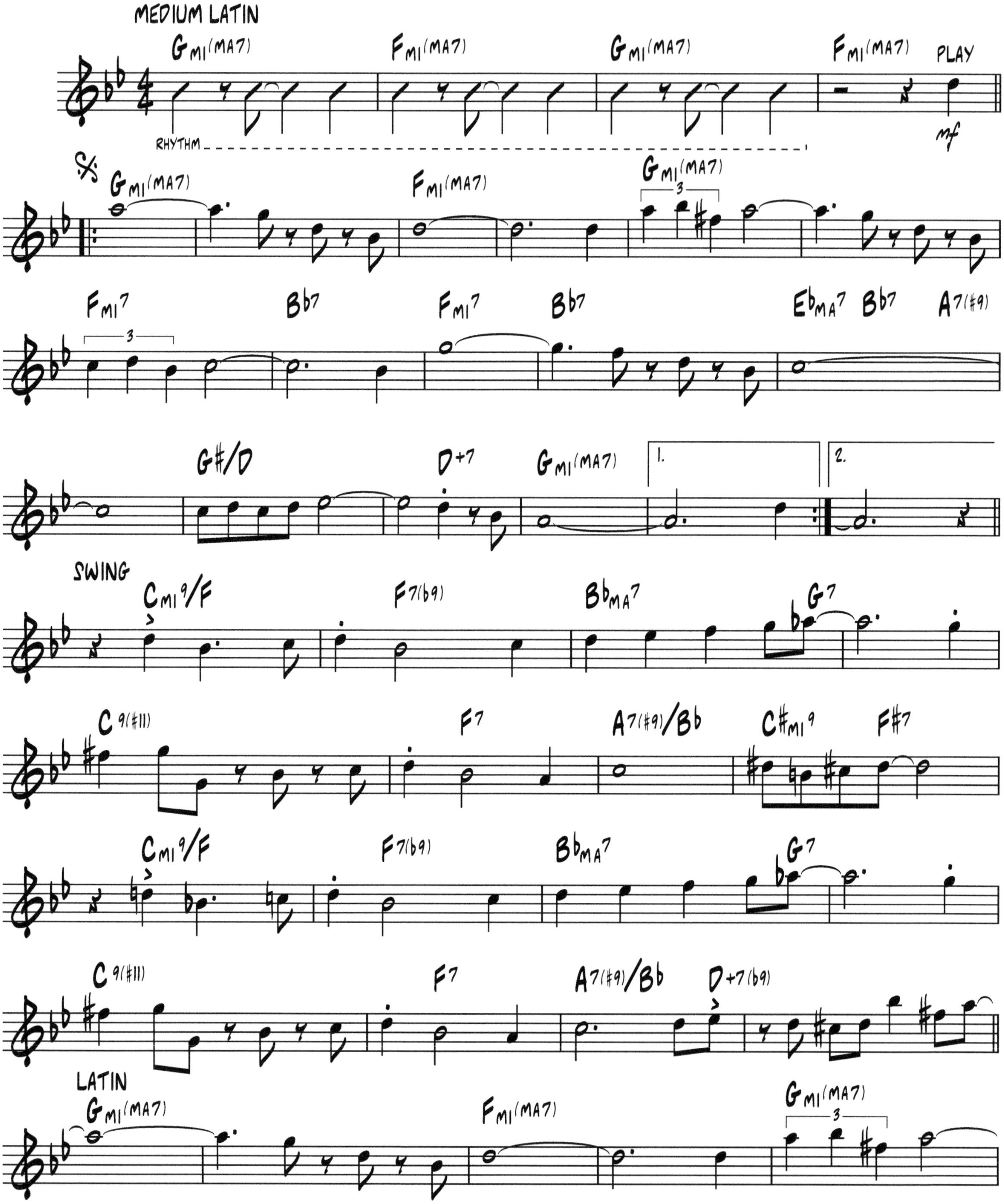

MEDIUM LATIN
GMI(MA7)
FMI(MA7)
GMI(MA7)
FMI(MA7)
PLAY
RHYTHM
mf
GMI(MA7)
FMI(MA7)
GMI(MA7)
FMI7
Bb7
FMI7
Bb7
EbMA7
Bb7
A7(#9)
G#/D
D+7
GMI(MA7)
1.
2.
SWING
CMI9/F
F7(b9)
BbMA7
G7
C9(#11)
F7
A7(#9)/Bb
C#MI9
F#7
CMI9/F
F7(b9)
BbMA7
G7
C9(#11)
F7
A7(#9)/Bb
D+7(b9)
LATIN
GMI(MA7)
FMI(MA7)
GMI(MA7)

FMI7 Bb7 FMI7 Bb7
EbMA7 Bb7 A7(#9) G#/D TO CODA D+7 GMI(MA7)
SOLO
GMI(MA7) FMI(MA7) GMI(MA7)
FMI7 Bb7 FMI7 Bb7 EbMA7
A7(#9) G#/D D+7 GMI(MA7)
SWING
CMI7/F F7(b9) BbMA7 G7 C9(#11) F7
BbMA9 C#MI9 F#7 CMI7/F F7(b9) BbMA7 G7
C9(#11) F7 BbMA7 D+7(b9) LATIN GMI(MA7)
FMI(MA7) GMI(MA7) FMI7 Bb7 FMI7
Bb7 EbMA7 A7(#9) G#/D D+7 GMI(MA7) D.S. AL CODA PLAY
mf
CODA D+7 GMI(MA7)

CD

7: SPLIT TRACK/MELODY

8: FULL STEREO TRACK

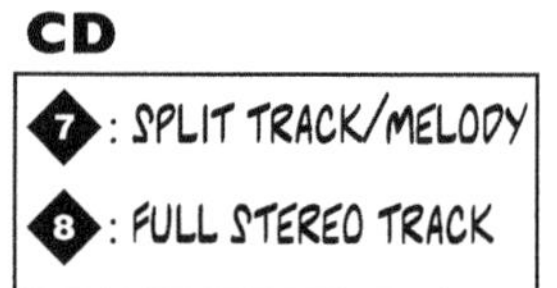

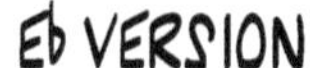

OPUS DE FUNK

WORDS AND MUSIC BY
HORACE SILVER

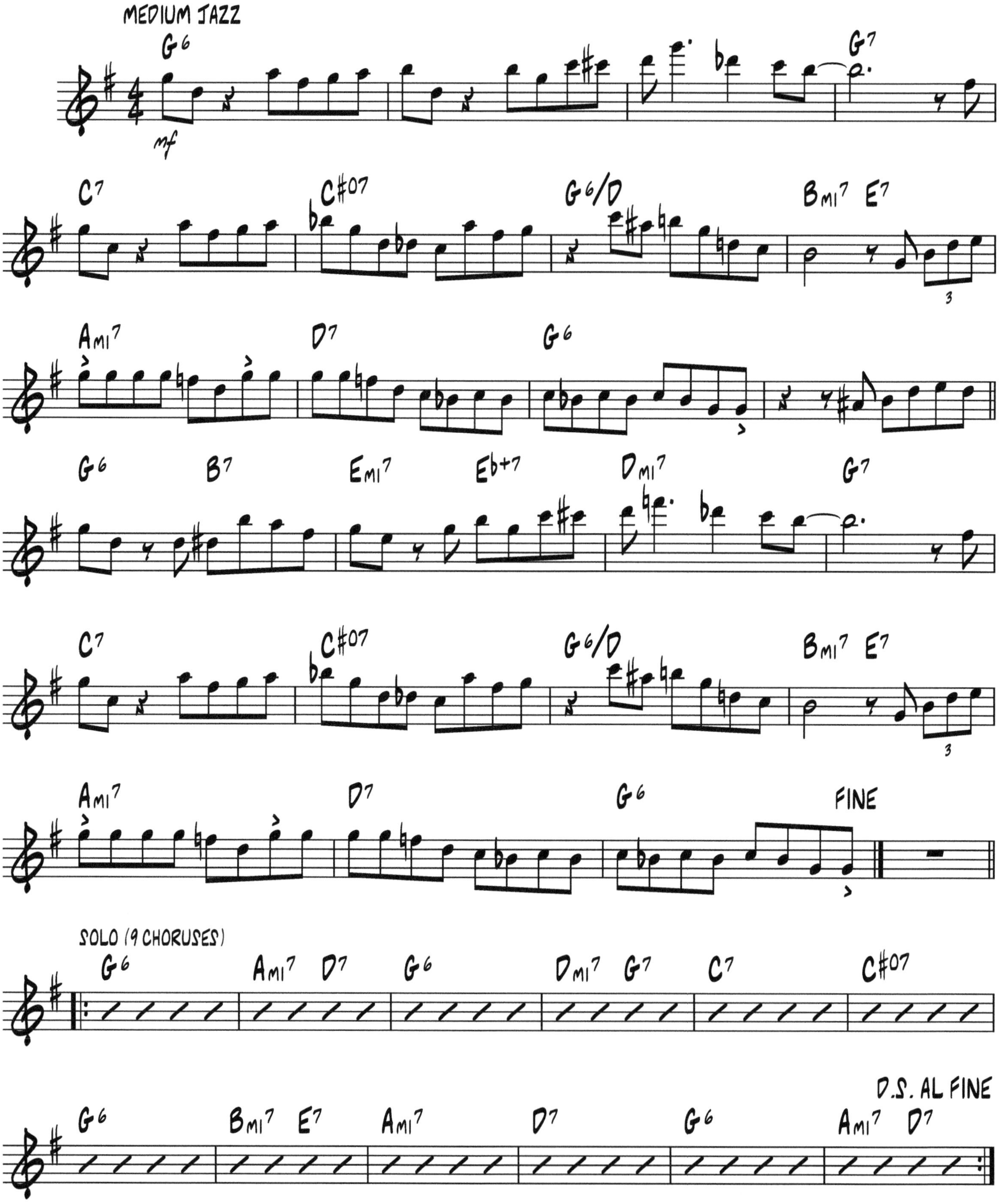

E♭ VERSION

MEDIUM JAZZ
G6
mf
G7
C7
C#o7
G6/D
Bmi7 E7
3
Ami7
D7
G6
G6
B7
Emi7
E♭+7
Dmi7
G7
C7
C#o7
G6/D
Bmi7 E7
3
Ami7
D7
G6
FINE
SOLO (9 CHORUSES)
G6
Ami7 D7
G6
Dmi7 G7
C7
C#o7
D.S. AL FINE
G6
Bmi7 E7
Ami7
D7
G6
Ami7 D7

PEACE

CD
9 : SPLIT TRACK/MELODY
10 : FULL STEREO TRACK
E♭ VERSION
WORDS AND MUSIC BY
HORACE SILVER
SLOW BALLAD
F♯MI7(♭5) F9 EMI7 A7(♭9) G♯MA7 AMI7(♭5) D+7(♯9)
GMA7 G♯MI7 C♯9 F♯MA7 D♯MI7
TO CODA
CMI7(♭5) F13 F+7 B♭MA7 A7(♭5) G♯7(♭5) GMA7 GMA7
SOLO
F♯MI7(♭5) F9 EMI7 A7(♭9) G♯MA7 AMI7(♭5) D+7(♯9)
GMA7 G♯MI7 C♯9 F♯MA7 D♯MI7
D.S. AL CODA
CMI7(♭5) F13 F+7 B♭MA7 A7(♭5) G♯7(♭5) GMA7
CODA
GMA9

CD
11 : SPLIT TRACK/MELODY
12 : FULL STEREO TRACK
THE PREACHER
WORDS AND MUSIC BY
HORACE SILVER
E♭ VERSION
SWING
A7
D6
D7
G7
G#07
D6/A
A9
E9
G9
F#9
TO CODA
B7(#9)
E7
A9SUS
A7(b9)
1.
2.
SOLO
1.-4.
5.
D.S. AL CODA
TAKE REPEAT
PLAY
CODA
D13

SISTER SADIE

WORDS AND MUSIC BY
HORACE SILVER

CD

13: SPLIT TRACK/MELODY

14: FULL STEREO TRACK

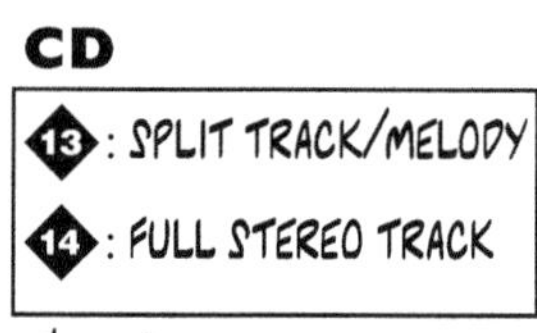

SEÑOR BLUES

WORDS AND MUSIC BY
HORACE SILVER

E♭ VERSION

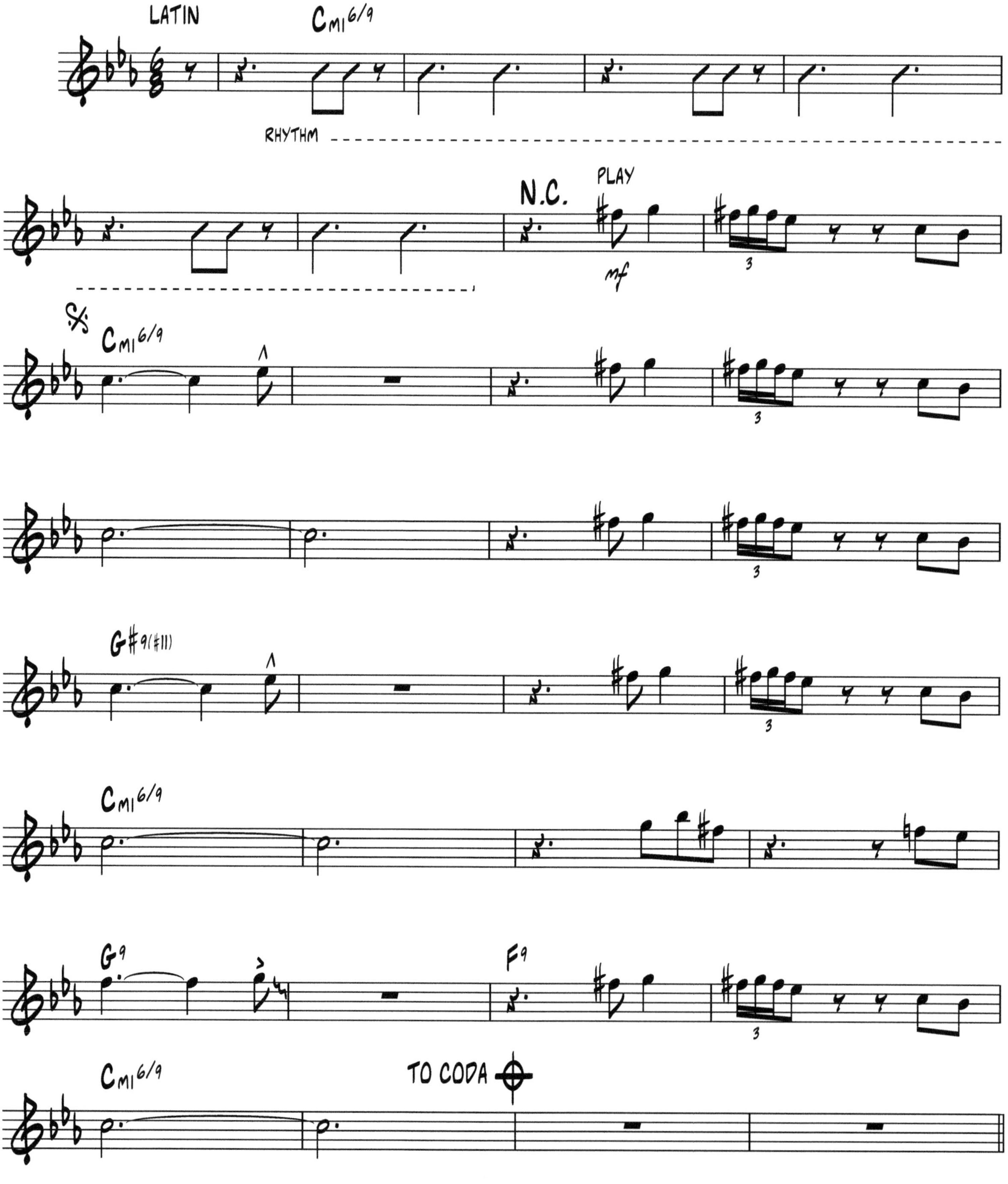

LATIN
Cmi6/9
RHYTHM
N.C.
PLAY
mf
3
Cmi6/9
3
3
G#9(#11)
3
Cmi6/9
G9
F9
3
Cmi6/9
TO CODA

SOLO
Cmi6/9
G#9(#11)
Cmi6/9
G13
F13
Cmi6/9
1., 2.
3.
PLAY
mf
D.S. AL CODA
CODA
Cmi6/9
RHYTHM

E♭ VERSION

WORDS AND MUSIC BY
HORACE SILVER

MEDIUM LATIN

3 Dmi9 mf

C9 Bb9 A9 Dmi9 1.

2. C9 Dmi9

C9 Bb9 A9 TO CODA Dmi9

SOLOS (2 CHORUSES)

Dmi9 C9 Bb9

A9 Dmi9 1. 2. C9

D.S. AL CODA
TAKE REPEAT
LAST TIME

Dmi9 C9 Bb9 A9 Dmi9 mf

CODA

Dmi9

RHYTHM

CD
19: SPLIT TRACK/MELODY
20: FULL STEREO TRACK
STROLLIN'
WORDS AND MUSIC BY
HORACE SILVER
Eb VERSION
MEDIUM SWING
PLAY
PIANO
BASS
mf
TO CODA
SOLO
D.S. AL CODA
TAKE REPEAT
CODA

DOODLIN'

WORDS AND MUSIC BY
HORACE SILVER

THE JODY GRIND

CD

5 : SPLIT TRACK/MELODY

6 : FULL STEREO TRACK

NICA'S DREAM

Abmi7 Db7 Abmi7 Db7
Gbma7 Db7 C7(#9) B/F TO CODA F+7 Bbmi(MA7)
SOLO
Bbmi(MA7) Abmi(MA7) Bbmi(MA7)
Abmi7 Db7 Abmi7 Db7 Gbma7
C7(#9) B/F F+7 Bbmi(MA7)
SWING
Ebmi7/Ab Ab7(b9) Dbma7 Bb7 Eb9(#11) Ab7
Dbma9 Emi9 A7 Ebmi7/Ab Ab7(b9) Dbma7 Bb7
Eb9(#11) Ab7 Dbma7 F+7(b9) LATIN Bbmi(MA7)
Abmi(MA7) Bbmi(MA7) Abmi7 Db7 Abmi7
Db7 Gbma7 C7(#9) B/F F+7 Bbmi(MA7) D.S. AL CODA PLAY
mf
CODA F+7 Bbmi(MA7)

OPUS DE FUNK

CD
: SPLIT TRACK/MELODY
8 : FULL STEREO TRACK
WORDS AND MUSIC BY
HORACE SILVER
C VERSION
MEDIUM JAZZ
Bb6
mf
Bb7
Eb7
E07
Bb6/F
DMI7 G7
3
CMI7
F7
Bb6
Bb6
D7
GMI7
Gb+7
FMI7
Bb7
Eb7
E07
Bb6/F
DMI7 G7
3
CMI7
F7
Bb6
FINE
SOLO (9 CHORUSES)
Bb6
CMI7 F7
Bb6
FMI7 Bb7
Eb7
E07
D.S. AL FINE
Bb6
DMI7 G7
CMI7
F7
Bb6
CMI7 F7

CD
9 : SPLIT TRACK/MELODY
10 : FULL STEREO TRACK
PEACE
WORDS AND MUSIC BY
HORACE SILVER
C VERSION
SLOW BALLAD
Ami7(b5) Ab9 Gmi7 C7(b9) Bma7 Cmi7(b5) F+7(#9)
mf
Bbma7 Bmi7 E9 Ama7 F#mi7
Ebmi7(b5) Ab13 Ab+7 Dbma7 C7(b5) B7(b5)
TO CODA
1. Bbma7
2. Bbma7
SOLO
Ami7(b5) Ab9 Gmi7 C7(b9) Bma7 Cmi7(b5) F+7(#9)
Bbma7 Bmi7 E9 Ama7 F#mi7
D.S. AL CODA
Ebmi7(b5) Ab13 Ab+7 Dbma7 C7(b5) B7(b5) Bbma7
mf
CODA
Bbma9

CD
11 : SPLIT TRACK/MELODY
12 : FULL STEREO TRACK
THE PREACHER
WORDS AND MUSIC BY
HORACE SILVER
C VERSION
SWING
C7 F6 F7 Bb7 B07
mf
F6/C C9 F6 G9 C9
F6 F7 Bb9 A9 Bb9 B07
TO CODA
F6/C D7(#9) G7 C9SUS C7(b9) F6 1. C9 2. F6 C9
SOLO
F6 F7 Bb7 B07 F6/C C9 F6
G9 C9 F6 F7 Bb9 A9 Bb9 B07
F6/C D7(#9) 1.-4. G7 C7(b9) F6 C9 5. G7 C7(b9) F6 C9
D.S. AL CODA
TAKE REPEAT
PLAY
mf
CODA
F13

SISTER SADIE

9: C VERSION

SEÑOR BLUES

WORDS AND MUSIC BY
HORACE SILVER

LATIN

E♭MI6/9

RHYTHM

N.C.

PLAY

mf

3

E♭MI6/9

B9(♯11)

E♭MI6/9

B♭9

A♭9

E♭MI6/9

TO CODA

SOLO
Eb MI 6/9
B 9(#11)
Eb MI 6/9
Bb13
Ab13
Eb MI 6/9
1., 2.
3.
PLAY
mf
D.S. AL CODA
CODA
Eb MI 6/9
RHYTHM

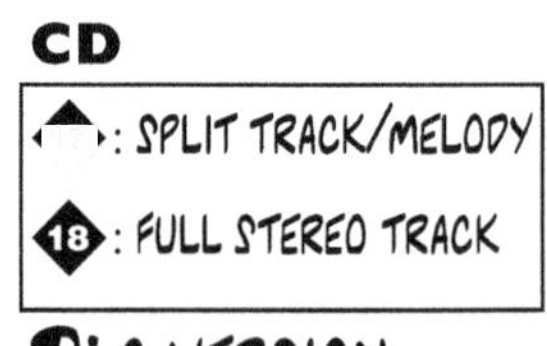

CD
: SPLIT TRACK/MELODY
18 : FULL STEREO TRACK

C VERSION

SONG FOR MY FATHER

WORDS AND MUSIC BY
HORACE SILVER

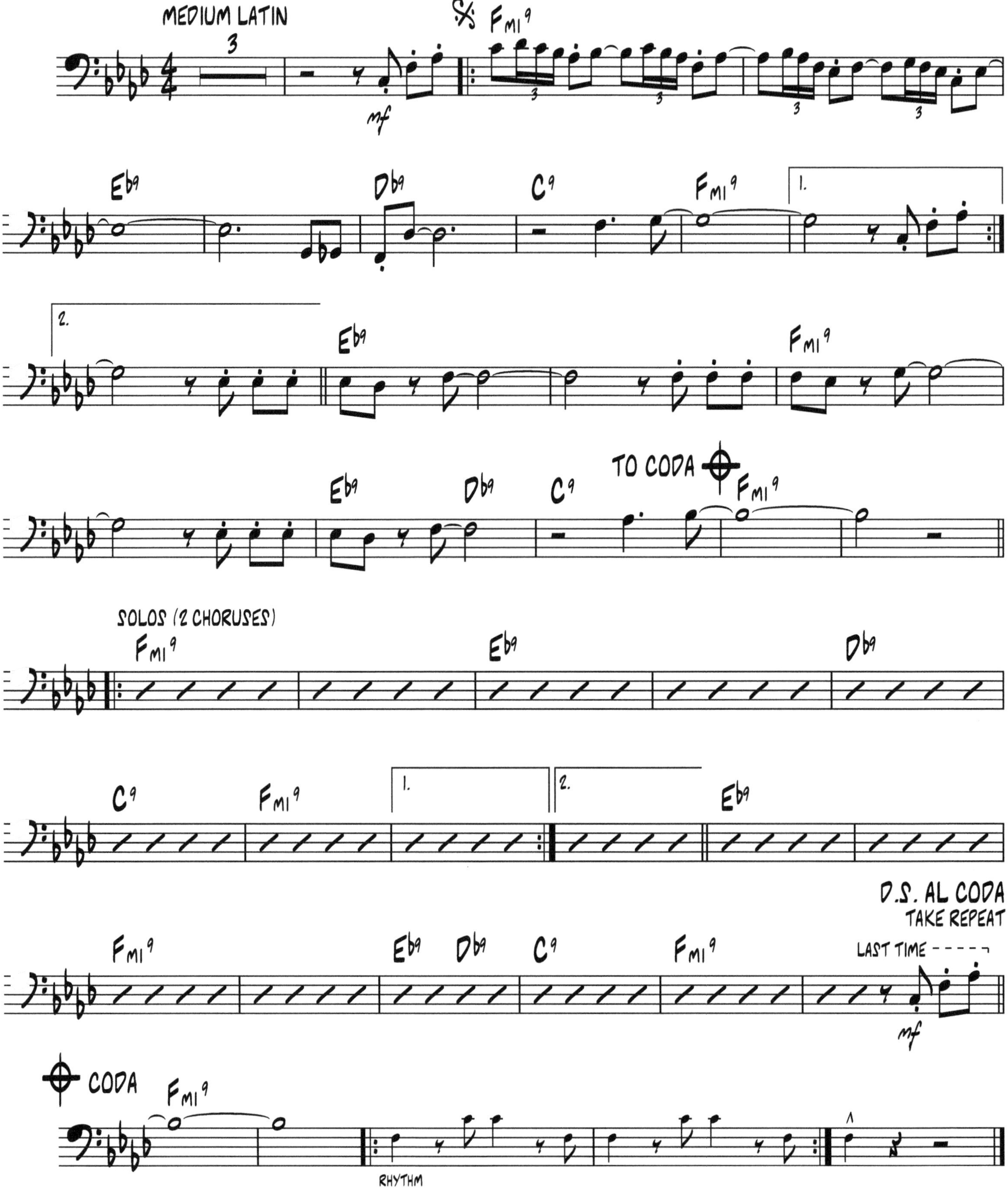

MEDIUM LATIN
3
mf
FMI9
Eb9
Db9
C9
FMI9
1.
2.
Eb9
FMI9
Eb9
Db9
C9
TO CODA
FMI9
SOLOS (2 CHORUSES)
FMI9
Eb9
Db9
C9
FMI9
1.
2.
Eb9
D.S. AL CODA
TAKE REPEAT
FMI9
Eb9
Db9
C9
FMI9
LAST TIME
mf
CODA
FMI9
RHYTHM

CD
19 : SPLIT TRACK/MELODY
20 : FULL STEREO TRACK
STROLLIN'
WORDS AND MUSIC BY
HORACE SILVER
C VERSION
MEDIUM SWING
PLAY
PIANO
BASS
mf
TO CODA
SOLO
D.S. AL CODA
TAKE REPEAT
CODA

Presenting the Hal Leonard JAZZ PLAY-ALONG® SERIES

1. DUKE ELLINGTON
00841644 $16.95

1A. MAIDEN VOYAGE/ALL BLUES
00843158 $15.99

2. MILES DAVIS
00841645 $16.95

3. THE BLUES
00841646 $16.99

4. JAZZ BALLADS
00841691 $16.99

5. BEST OF BEBOP
00841689 $16.99

6. JAZZ CLASSICS WITH EASY CHANGES
00841690 $16.99

7. ESSENTIAL JAZZ STANDARDS
00843000 $16.99

8. ANTONIO CARLOS JOBIM AND THE ART OF THE BOSSA NOVA
00843001 $16.95

9. DIZZY GILLESPIE
00843002 $16.99

10. DISNEY CLASSICS
00843003 $16.99

11. RODGERS AND HART – FAVORITES
00843004 $16.99

12. ESSENTIAL JAZZ CLASSICS
00843005 $16.99

13. JOHN COLTRANE
00843006 $16.95

14. IRVING BERLIN
00843007 $15.99

15. RODGERS & HAMMERSTEIN
00843008 $15.99

16. COLE PORTER
00843009 $15.95

17. COUNT BASIE
00843010 $16.95

18. HAROLD ARLEN
00843011 $15.95

19. COOL JAZZ
00843012 $15.95

20. CHRISTMAS CAROLS
00843080 $14.95

21. RODGERS AND HART – CLASSICS
00843014 $14.95

22. WAYNE SHORTER
00843015 $16.95

23. LATIN JAZZ
00843016 $16.95

24. EARLY JAZZ STANDARDS
00843017 $14.95

25. CHRISTMAS JAZZ
00843018 $16.95

26. CHARLIE PARKER
00843019 $16.95

27. GREAT JAZZ STANDARDS
00843020 $15.99

28. BIG BAND ERA
00843021 $15.99

29. LENNON AND McCARTNEY
00843022 $16.95

30. BLUES' BEST
00843023 $15.99

31. JAZZ IN THREE
00843024 $15.99

32. BEST OF SWING
00843025 $15.99

33. SONNY ROLLINS
00843029 $15.95

34. ALL TIME STANDARDS
00843030 $15.99

35. BLUESY JAZZ
00843031 $15.99

36. HORACE SILVER
00843032 $16.99

37. BILL EVANS
00843033 $16.95

38. YULETIDE JAZZ
00843034 $16.95

39. "ALL THE THINGS YOU ARE" & MORE JEROME KERN SONGS
00843035 $15.99

40. BOSSA NOVA
00843036 $15.99

41. CLASSIC DUKE ELLINGTON
00843037 $16.99

42. GERRY MULLIGAN – FAVORITES
00843038 $16.99

43. GERRY MULLIGAN – CLASSICS
00843039 $16.95

44. OLIVER NELSON
00843040 $16.95

45. JAZZ AT THE MOVIES
00843041 $15.99

46. BROADWAY JAZZ STANDARDS
00843042 $15.99

47. CLASSIC JAZZ BALLADS
00843043 $15.99

48. BEBOP CLASSICS
00843044 $16.99

49. MILES DAVIS – STANDARDS
00843045 $16.95

50. GREAT JAZZ CLASSICS
00843046 $15.99

51. UP-TEMPO JAZZ
00843047 $15.99

52. STEVIE WONDER
00843048 $15.95

53. RHYTHM CHANGES
00843049 $15.99

54. "MOONLIGHT IN VERMONT" & OTHER GREAT STANDARDS
00843050 $15.99

55. BENNY GOLSON
00843052 $15.95

56. "GEORGIA ON MY MIND" & OTHER SONGS BY HOAGY CARMICHAEL
00843056 $15.99

57. VINCE GUARALDI
00843057 $16.99

58. MORE LENNON AND McCARTNEY
00843059 $15.99

59. SOUL JAZZ
00843060 $15.99

60. DEXTER GORDON
00843061 $15.95

61. MONGO SANTAMARIA
00843062 $15.95

62. JAZZ-ROCK FUSION
00843063 $14.95

63. CLASSICAL JAZZ
00843064 $14.95

64. TV TUNES
00843065 $14.95

65. SMOOTH JAZZ
00843066 $16.99

66. A CHARLIE BROWN CHRISTMAS
00843067 $16.99

67. CHICK COREA
00843068 $15.95

68. CHARLES MINGUS
00843069 $16.95

69. CLASSIC JAZZ
00843071 $15.99

70. THE DOORS
00843072 $14.95

71. COLE PORTER CLASSICS
00843073 $14.95

72. CLASSIC JAZZ BALLADS
00843074 $15.99

73. JAZZ/BLUES
00843075 $14.95

74. BEST JAZZ CLASSICS
00843076 $15.99

75. PAUL DESMOND
00843077 $14.95

76. BROADWAY JAZZ BALLADS
00843078 $15.99

77. JAZZ ON BROADWAY
00843079 $15.99

78. STEELY DAN
00843070 $14.99

79. MILES DAVIS – CLASSICS
00843081 $15.99

80. JIMI HENDRIX
00843083 $15.99

81. FRANK SINATRA – CLASSICS
00843084 $15.99

82. FRANK SINATRA – STANDARDS
00843085 $15.99

83. ANDREW LLOYD WEBBER
00843104 $14.95

84. BOSSA NOVA CLASSICS
00843105 $14.95

85. MOTOWN HITS
00843109 $14.95

86. BENNY GOODMAN
00843110 $14.95

87. DIXIELAND
00843111 $14.95

88. DUKE ELLINGTON FAVORITES
00843112 $14.95

89. IRVING BERLIN FAVORITES
00843113 $14.95

90. THELONIOUS MONK CLASSICS
00841262 $16.99

91. THELONIOUS MONK FAVORITES
00841263 $16.99

92. LEONARD BERNSTEIN
00450134 $15.99

93. DISNEY FAVORITES
00843142 $14.99

94. RAY
00843143 $14.99

95. JAZZ AT THE LOUNGE
00843144 $14.99

96. LATIN JAZZ STANDARDS
00843145 $14.99

97. MAYBE I'M AMAZED
00843148 $15.99

98. DAVE FRISHBERG
00843149 $15.99

99. SWINGING STANDARDS
00843150 $14.99

100. LOUIS ARMSTRONG
00740423 $15.99

101. BUD POWELL
00843152 $14.99

102. JAZZ POP
00843153 $14.99

103. ON GREEN DOLPHIN STREET & OTHER JAZZ CLASSICS
00843154 $14.99

104. ELTON JOHN
00843155 $14.99

105. SOULFUL JAZZ
00843151 $15.99

106. SLO' JAZZ
00843117 $14.99

107. MOTOWN CLASSICS
00843116 $14.99

108. JAZZ WALTZ
00843159 $15.99

109. OSCAR PETERSON
00843160 $15.99

110. JUST STANDARDS
00843161 $15.99

111. COOL CHRISTMAS
00843162 $15.99

114. MODERN JAZZ QUARTET FAVORITES
00843163 $15.99

115. THE SOUND OF MUSIC
00843164 $15.99

116. JACO PASTORIUS
00843165 $15.99

117. ANTONIO CARLOS JOBIM – MORE HITS
00843166 $15.99

118. BIG JAZZ STANDARDS COLLECTION
00843167 $27.50

119. JELLY ROLL MORTON
00843168 $15.99

120. J.S. BACH
00843169 $15.99

121. DJANGO REINHARDT
00843170 $15.99

122. PAUL SIMON
00843182 $16.99

123. BACHARACH & DAVID
00843185 $15.99

124. JAZZ-ROCK HORN HITS
00843186 $15.99

126. COUNT BASIE CLASSICS
00843157 $15.99

Prices, contents, and availability subject to change without notice.

FOR MORE INFORMATION, SEE YOUR LOCAL MUSIC DEALER, OR WRITE TO:

HAL•LEONARD®
CORPORATION
7777 W. BLUEMOUND RD. P.O. BOX 13819
MILWAUKEE, WISCONSIN 53213

Visit Hal Leonard online at
www.halleonard.com
for complete songlists.

0910

ARTIST TRANSCRIPTIONS®

Artist Transcriptions are authentic, note-for-note transcriptions of today's hottest artists in jazz, pop and rock. These outstanding, accurate arrangements are in an easy-to-read format which includes all essential lines. **Artist Transcriptions** can be used to perform, sequence or for reference.

CLARINET

00672423 Buddy De Franco Collection $19.95

FLUTE

00672379 Eric Dolphy Collection..........................$19.95
00672582 The Very Best of James Galway $16.99
00672372 James Moody Collection – Sax and Flute $19.95

GUITAR & BASS

00660113 The Guitar Style of George Benson.......$16.99
00699072 Guitar Book of Pierre Bensusan $29.95
00672331 Ron Carter – Acoustic Bass.................$19.99
00672573 Ray Brown – Legendary Jazz Bassist ..$19.99
00672307 Stanley Clarke Collection.....................$19.99
00660115 Al Di Meola – Friday Night in San Francisco...............$16.99
00604043 Al Di Meola – Music, Words, Pictures $14.95
00672574 Al Di Meola – Pursuit of Radical Rhapsody $22.99
00125617 Best of Herb Ellis $19.99
00673245 Jazz Style of Tal Farlow $19.99
00699306 Jim Hall – Exploring Jazz Guitar...........$19.99
00604049 Allan Holdsworth – Reaching for the Uncommon Chord $17.99
00699215 Leo Kottke – Eight Songs.................... $17.99
00672353 Joe Pass Collection $19.99
00673216 John Patitucci...................................... $17.99
00027083 Django Reinhardt Anthology $16.99
00672374 Johnny Smith Guitar Solos....................$19.99

PIANO & KEYBOARD

00672338 Monty Alexander Collection $19.95
00672487 Monty Alexander Plays Standards $19.95
00672520 Count Basie Collection $19.95
00192307 Bebop Piano Legends..........................$19.99
00113680 Blues Piano Legends............................$19.99
00278003 A Charlie Brown Christmas................. $17.99
00672439 Cyrus Chestnut Collection $19.95
00672300 Chick Corea – Paint the World.............$16.99
14037739 Storyville Presents Duke Ellington $19.99
00146105 Bill Evans – Alone................................ $17.99
00672537 Bill Evans at Town Hall..........................$19.99
00672548 The Mastery of Bill Evans $16.99
00672425 Bill Evans – Piano Interpretations........ $22.99
00672365 Bill Evans – Piano Standards................$19.99
00121885 Bill Evans – Time Remembered $19.99
00672510 Bill Evans Trio – Vol. 1: 1959-1961 .... $24.95
00672511 Bill Evans Trio – Vol. 2: 1962-1965........ $24.99
00672512 Bill Evans Trio – Vol. 3: 1968-1974........ $24.99
00672513 Bill Evans Trio – Vol. 4: 1979-1980 .... $24.95
00672381 Tommy Flanagan Collection................ $24.99
00193332 Erroll Garner – Concert by the Sea.......$19.99
00672492 Benny Goodman Collection $16.95
00672486 Vince Guaraldi Collection......................$19.99
00672419 Herbie Hancock Collection....................$19.95
00672438 Hampton Hawes $19.95
14037738 Storyville Presents Earl Hines...............$19.99
00672322 Ahmad Jamal Collection $24.99
00255671 Jazz Piano Masterpieces......................$19.99
00124367 Jazz Piano Masters Play Rodgers & Hammerstein $19.99
00672564 Best of Jeff Lorber............................... $17.99
00672476 Brad Mehldau Collection.......................$19.99
00672388 Best of Thelonious Monk $19.95
00672389 Thelonious Monk Collection................. $22.99
00672390 Thelonious Monk Plays Jazz Standards – Volume 1 ....$19.99
00672391 Thelonious Monk Plays Jazz Standards – Volume 2 ....$19.95
00672433 Jelly Roll Morton – The Piano Rolls $16.99
00672553 Charlie Parker for Piano........................$19.95
00672542 Oscar Peterson – Jazz Piano Solos..... $17.99
00672562 Oscar Peterson – A Jazz Portrait of Frank Sinatra...........$19.95
00264094 Oscar Peterson – Night Train $19.99
00672544 Oscar Peterson – Originals..................$10.99
00672532 Oscar Peterson – Plays Broadway........$19.95
00672531 Oscar Peterson – Plays Duke Ellington $24.99
00672563 Oscar Peterson – A Royal Wedding Suite $19.99
00672569 Oscar Peterson – Tracks.......................$19.99
00672533 Oscar Peterson – Trios........................ $24.95
00672543 Oscar Peterson Trio – Canadiana Suite $12.99
00672534 Very Best of Oscar Peterson............... $22.95
00672371 Bud Powell Classics.............................$19.99
00672376 Bud Powell Collection $19.95
00672507 Gonzalo Rubalcaba Collection $19.95
00672303 Horace Silver Collection...................... $22.99
00672316 Art Tatum Collection $24.99
00672355 Art Tatum Solo Book $19.95
00673215 McCoy Tyner $19.99
00672321 Cedar Walton Collection $19.95
00672519 Kenny Werner Collection......................$19.95
00672434 Teddy Wilson Collection $19.95

SAXOPHONE

00672566 The Mindi Abair Collection $14.99
00673244 Julian "Cannonball" Adderley Collection.............................$19.95
00673237 Michael Brecker $19.95
00672429 Michael Brecker Collection $22.99
00672315 Benny Carter Plays Standards............ $22.95
00672394 James Carter Collection.......................$19.95
00672349 John Coltrane Plays Giant Steps $19.95
00672529 John Coltrane – Giant Steps.................$17.99
00672494 John Coltrane – A Love Supreme $15.99
00307393 John Coltrane – Omnibook: C Instruments $24.99
00307391 John Coltrane – Omnibook: B-flat Instruments $27.99
00307392 John Coltrane – Omnibook: E-flat Instruments $29.99
00307394 John Coltrane – Omnibook: Bass Clef Instruments $24.99
00672493 John Coltrane Plays "Coltrane Changes"....................$19.95
00672453 John Coltrane Plays Standards........... $22.99
00673233 John Coltrane Solos $22.95
00672328 Paul Desmond Collection.....................$19.99
00672379 Eric Dolphy Collection..........................$19.95
00672530 Kenny Garrett Collection $19.95
00699375 Stan Getz...$19.99
00672377 Stan Getz – Bossa Novas $22.99
00672375 Stan Getz – Standards.........................$19.99
00673254 Great Tenor Sax Solos.........................$18.99
00672523 Coleman Hawkins Collection $19.99
00673252 Joe Henderson – Selections from "Lush Life" & "So Near So Far".............$19.95
00673239 Best of Kenny G...................................$19.95
00673229 Kenny G – Breathless $19.95
00672462 Kenny G – Classics in the Key of G $19.95
00672485 Kenny G – Faith: A Holiday Album $15.99
00672373 Kenny G – The Moment.......................$19.95
00672498 Jackie McLean Collection $19.95
00672372 James Moody Collection – Sax and Flute $19.95
00672416 Frank Morgan Collection $19.95
00672539 Gerry Mulligan Collection.....................$19.95
00672352 Charlie Parker Collection $19.95
00672561 Best of Sonny Rollins...........................$19.95
00102751 Sonny Rollins with the Modern Jazz Quartet $17.99
00675000 David Sanborn Collection $19.99
00672491 New Best of Wayne Shorter................ $22.99
00672550 The Sonny Stitt Collection....................$19.95
00672524 Lester Young Collection........................$19.99

TROMBONE

00672332 J.J. Johnson Collection $19.99
00672489 Steve Turré Collection $19.99

TRUMPET

00672557 Herb Alpert Collection $17.99
00672480 Louis Armstrong Collection $19.99
00672481 Louis Armstrong Plays Standards........ $19.99
00672435 Chet Baker Collection $19.99
00672556 Best of Chris Botti $19.99
00672448 Miles Davis – Originals, Vol. 1 ....$19.95
00672451 Miles Davis – Originals, Vol. 2 ....$19.95
00672450 Miles Davis – Standards, Vol. 1 ....$19.99
00672449 Miles Davis – Standards, Vol. 2 ....$19.95
00672479 Dizzy Gillespie Collection $19.95
00673214 Freddie Hubbard $19.99
00672382 Tom Harrell – Jazz Trumpet $19.95
00672363 Jazz Trumpet Solos............................... $9.95
00672506 Chuck Mangione Collection $19.95
00672525 Arturo Sandoval – Trumpet Evolution....$19.99

7777 W. Bluemound Rd. P.O. Box 13819 Milwaukee, WI 53213

Visit our web site for a complete listing of our titles with songlists at
www.halleonard.com

Prices, content, and availability subject to change without notice.

Jazz Instruction & Improvisation

BOOKS FOR ALL INSTRUMENTS FROM HAL LEONARD

AN APPROACH TO JAZZ IMPROVISATION

by Dave Pozzi
Musicians Institute Press

Explore the styles of Charlie Parker, Sonny Rollins, Bud Powell and others with this comprehensive guide to jazz improvisation. Covers: scale choices • chord analysis • phrasing • melodies • harmonic progressions • more.

00695135 Book/CD Pack....................................$17.95

THE ART OF MODULATING

FOR PIANISTS AND JAZZ MUSICIANS

by Carlos Salzedo & Lucile Lawrence
Schirmer

The Art of Modulating is a treatise originally intended for the harp, but this edition has been edited for use by intermediate keyboardists and other musicians who have an understanding of basic music theory. In its pages you will find: table of intervals; modulation rules; modulation formulas; examples of modulation; extensions and cadences; ten fragments of dances; five characteristic pieces; and more.

50490581 ....$19.99

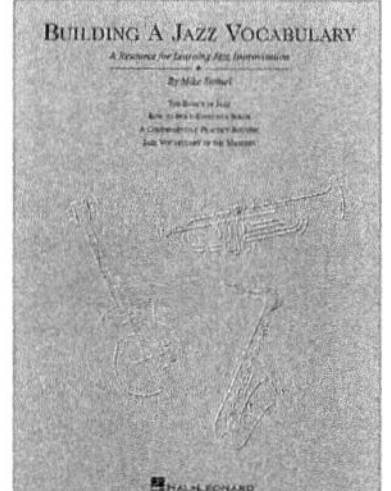

BUILDING A JAZZ VOCABULARY

By Mike Steinel

A valuable resource for learning the basics of jazz from Mike Steinel of the University of North Texas. It covers: the basics of jazz • how to build effective solos • a comprehensive practice routine • and a jazz vocabulary of the masters.

00849911 ....$19.99

THE CYCLE OF FIFTHS

by Emile and Laura De Cosmo

This essential instruction book provides more than 450 exercises, including hundreds of melodic and rhythmic ideas. The book is designed to help improvisors master the cycle of fifths, one of the primary progressions in music. Guaranteed to refine technique, enhance improvisational fluency, and improve sight-reading!

00311114 ....$16.99

THE DIATONIC CYCLE

by Emile and Laura De Cosmo

Renowned jazz educators Emile and Laura De Cosmo provide more than 300 exercises to help improvisors tackle one of music's most common progressions: the diatonic cycle. This book is guaranteed to refine technique, enhance improvisational fluency, and improve sight-reading!

00311115 ....$16.95

EAR TRAINING

by Keith Wyatt, Carl Schroeder and Joe Elliott
Musicians Institute Press

Covers: basic pitch matching • singing major and minor scales • identifying intervals • transcribing melodies and rhythm • identifying chords and progressions • seventh chords and the blues • modal interchange, chromaticism, modulation • and more.

00695198 Book/Online Audio $24.99

EXERCISES AND ETUDES FOR THE JAZZ INSTRUMENTALIST

by J.J. Johnson

Designed as study material and playable by any instrument, these pieces run the gamut of the jazz experience, featuring common and uncommon time signatures and keys, and styles from ballads to funk. They are progressively graded so that both beginners and professionals will be challenged by the demands of this wonderful music.

00842018 Bass Clef Edition $19.99
00842042 Treble Clef Edition $16.95

JAZZOLOGY

THE ENCYCLOPEDIA OF JAZZ THEORY FOR ALL MUSICIANS

by Robert Rawlins and Nor Eddine Bahha

This comprehensive resource covers a variety of jazz topics, for beginners and pros of any instrument. The book serves as an encyclopedia for reference, a thorough methodology for the student, and a workbook for the classroom.

00311167 ....$19.99

JAZZ THEORY RESOURCES

by Bert Ligon
Houston Publishing, Inc.

This is a jazz theory text in two volumes. **Volume 1 includes:** review of basic theory • rhythm in jazz performance • triadic generalization • diatonic harmonic progressions and analysis • substitutions and turnarounds • and more. **Volume 2 includes**: modes and modal frameworks • quartal harmony • extended tertian structures and triadic superimposition • pentatonic applications • coloring "outside" the lines and beyond • and more.

00030458 Volume 1 ....$39.99
00030459 Volume 2 ....$32.99

JOY OF IMPROV

by Dave Frank and John Amaral

This book/audio course on improvisation for all instruments and all styles will help players develop monster musical skills! Book One imparts a solid basis in technique, rhythm, chord theory, ear training and improv concepts. **Book Two** explores more advanced chord voicings, chord arranging techniques and more challenging blues and melodic lines. The audio can be used as a listening and play-along tool.

00220005 Book 1 – Book/Online Audio...............$27.99
00220006 Book 2 – Book/Online Audio...............$26.99

THE PATH TO JAZZ IMPROVISATION

by Emile and Laura De Cosmo

This fascinating jazz instruction book offers an innovative, scholarly approach to the art of improvisation. It includes in-depth analysis and lessons about: cycle of fifths • diatonic cycle • overtone series • pentatonic scale • harmonic and melodic minor scale • polytonal order of keys • blues and bebop scales • modes • and more.

00310904 ....$19.99

THE SOURCE

THE DICTIONARY OF CONTEMPORARY AND TRADITIONAL SCALES

by Steve Barta

This book serves as an informative guide for people who are looking for good, solid information regarding scales, chords, and how they work together. It provides right and left hand fingerings for scales, chords, and complete inversions. Includes over 20 different scales, each written in all 12 keys.

00240885 ....$19.99

21 BEBOP EXERCISES

by Steve Rawlins

This book/CD pack is both a warm-up collection and a manual for bebop phrasing. Its tasty and sophisticated exercises will help you develop your proficiency with jazz interpretation. It concentrates on practice in all twelve keys – moving higher by half-step – to help develop dexterity and range. The companion CD includes all of the exercises in 12 keys.

00315341 Book/CD Pack....................................$17.95

The Best-Selling Jazz Book of All Time Is Now Legal!

The Real Books are the most popular jazz books of all time. Since the 1970s, musicians have trusted these volumes to get them through every gig, night after night. The problem is that the books were illegally produced and distributed, without any regard to copyright law, or royalties paid to the composers who created these musical masterpieces.

Hal Leonard is very proud to present the first legitimate and legal editions of these books ever produced. You won't even notice the difference, other than all the notorious errors being fixed: the covers and typeface look the same, the song lists are nearly identical, and the price for our edition is even cheaper than the originals!

Every conscientious musician will appreciate that these books are now produced accurately and ethically, benefitting the songwriters that we owe for some of the greatest tunes of all time!

VOLUME 1

00240221 C Edition $39.99
00240224 B♭ Edition $39.99
00240225 E♭ Edition $39.99
00240226 Bass Clef Edition $39.99
00286389 F Edition $39.99
00240292 C Edition 6 x 9 ....$35.00
00240339 B♭ Edition 6 x 9 ....$35.00
00147792 Bass Clef Edition 6 x 9 ....$35.00
00451087 C Edition on CD-ROM $29.99
00200984 Online Backing Tracks: Selections $45.00
00110604 Book/USB Flash Drive Backing Tracks Pack $79.99
00110599 USB Flash Drive Only $50.00

VOLUME 2

00240222 C Edition $39.99
00240227 B♭ Edition $39.99
00240228 E♭ Edition $39.99
00240229 Bass Clef Edition $39.99
00240293 C Edition 6 x 9 ....$35.00
00125900 B♭ Edition 6 x 9 ....$35.00
00451088 C Edition on CD-ROM $30.99
00125900 The Real Book – Mini Edition $35.00
00204126 Backing Tracks on USB Flash Drive $50.00
00204131 C Edition – USB Flash Drive Pack $79.99

VOLUME 3

00240233 C Edition $39.99
00240284 B♭ Edition $39.99
00240285 E♭ Edition $39.99
00240286 Bass Clef Edition $39.99
00240338 C Edition 6 x 9 ....$35.00
00451089 C Edition on CD-ROM $29.99

VOLUME 4

00240296 C Edition $39.99
00103348 B♭ Edition $39.99
00103349 E♭ Edition $39.99
00103350 Bass Clef Edition $39.99

VOLUME 5

00240349 C Edition $39.99
00175278 B♭ Edition $39.99
00175279 E♭ Edition $39.99

VOLUME 6

00240534 C Edition $39.99
00223637 E♭ Edition $39.99

Also available:

00154230 The Real Bebop Book $34.99
00240264 The Real Blues Book $34.99
00310910 The Real Bluegrass Book $35.00
00240223 The Real Broadway Book $35.00
00240440 The Trane Book $22.99
00125426 The Real Country Book $39.99
00269721 The Real Miles Davis Book C Edition $24.99
00269723 The Real Miles Davis Book B♭ Edition $24.99
00240355 The Real Dixieland Book C Edition $32.50
00294853 The Real Dixieland Book E♭ Edition $35.00
00122335 The Real Dixieland Book B♭ Edition $35.00
00240235 The Duke Ellington Real Book $22.99
00240268 The Real Jazz Solos Book $30.00
00240348 The Real Latin Book C Edition $37.50
00127107 The Real Latin Book B♭ Edition $35.00
00120809 The Pat Metheny Real Book C Edition $27.50
00252119 The Pat Metheny Real Book B♭ Edition $24.99
00240358 The Charlie Parker Real Book C Edition $19.99
00275997 The Charlie Parker Real Book E♭ Edition $19.99
00118324 The Real Pop Book – Vol. 1 ....$35.00
00240331 The Bud Powell Real Book $19.99
00240437 The Real R&B Book C Edition $39.99
00276590 The Real R&B Book B♭ Edition $39.99
00240313 The Real Rock Book $35.00
00240323 The Real Rock Book – Vol. 2 ....$35.00
00240359 The Real Tab Book $32.50
00240317 The Real Worship Book $29.99

THE REAL CHRISTMAS BOOK

00240306 C Edition $32.50
00240345 B♭ Edition $32.50
00240346 E♭ Edition $35.00
00240347 Bass Clef Edition $32.50
00240431 A-G CD Backing Tracks $24.99
00240432 H-M CD Backing Tracks $24.99
00240433 N-Y CD Backing Tracks $24.99

THE REAL VOCAL BOOK

00240230 Volume 1 High Voice $35.00
00240307 Volume 1 Low Voice $35.00
00240231 Volume 2 High Voice $35.00
00240308 Volume 2 Low Voice $35.00
00240391 Volume 3 High Voice $35.00
00240392 Volume 3 Low Voice $35.00
00118318 Volume 4 High Voice $35.00
00118319 Volume 4 Low Voice $35.00

Complete song lists online at www.halleonard.com

Prices, content, and availability subject to change without notice.

0719
318